Presented to

_____

on

_____

by

_____

My First Communion
Bible

Written by Mary Martha Moss, FSP

Illustrated by Augusta Curreli

Pauline
BOOKS & MEDIA
Boston

Nihil Obstat: Reverend Thomas W. Buckley, S.T.D., S.S.L.

Imprimatur: ☩Seán Cardinal O'Malley, O.F.M. Cap.
Archbishop of Boston
July 13, 2017

ISBN 10: 0–8198–4965–0
ISBN 13: 978–0-8198–4965–6

Cover design by Mary Joseph Peterson, FSP

Cover art by Veronica Walsh

Illustrated by Augusta Curreli

Published by Pauline Books & Media, 50 Saint Pauls Avenue, Boston, MA 02130–3491

Printed in Korea

FCB SIPSKOGUNKYO9-15064 4965-0

www.pauline.org

Pauline Books & Media is the publishing house of the Daughters of St. Paul, an international congregation of women religious serving the Church with the communications media.

1 2 3 4 5 6 7 8 9   22 21 20 19 18

Contents

God Speaks to Us in the Bible

God loves us and wants us to know him. That is why he gives us the Bible, his word to us.

In the Old Testament, we read how God made the world and loves everyone in it. In the New Testament, we read about God's Son, Jesus. He came to save us from sin and show us the way to the Father.

Now that you can receive Jesus' Body and Blood in Holy Communion, it is good for you to also have your very own Bible. It will help you grow closer to God.

May God bless you and your whole family always.

1

2

Old Testament

God Made All Things

Genesis 1–2

Before the world began there was nothing—not one thing! There was only God. God made all things out of nothing.

First God said, "Let there be light," and there was light! Then God made the earth, the sky, and the sea. God filled the earth with all kinds of trees and plants. Next God made the sun, the moon, and the stars. God looked at all he had made and said, "It is good."

There were no sea animals yet, so God made dolphins, whales, and fish. God also made birds that fly in the sky. Then God made all sorts of land animals like cows, horses, and kangaroos. Some animals could be tamed, and some animals were wild. "It too is good," God said.

God loved all the things he had made, but he was not done yet. Then God made the first man and called him Adam. God put Adam in charge of the things on the earth, even the animals. Next God said, "Adam needs a helper, so he will not be alone." So, while Adam was asleep, God made the first woman. When Adam woke

6

up, he was so happy. "There she is at last!" he said. He called the woman Eve. God looked at them with love and blessed them. "It is all very good," God said.

After he made everything, God rested.

You made everything good, O God. Thank you for your gifts!

Adam and Eve

Genesis 2:15–17; 3

God loved Adam and Eve very much. He gave them a lovely garden and asked them to take care of it. God told Adam and Eve that

8

they could eat the fruit from all the trees except for the tree in the middle of the garden. "If you eat this fruit," God said, "you will die!"

One day the serpent came and spoke to Eve. He said, "Did God really tell you not to eat the fruit from this tree?"

"We can eat from every tree in the garden except this one," she told him. "If we eat its fruit, we will die."

"That's not true!" the serpent lied. "If you eat this fruit, you will know everything, just like God does!"

Eve chose to listen to the serpent. She took some of the fruit and ate it. Then she gave some to Adam, and he also ate it. Adam and Eve both disobeyed God. This was the first sin.

Because of their sin, Adam and Eve could not live in the garden any more. But God loved them so much, he gave Adam and Eve a special promise. God would send a Savior one day to save them from sin.

God, may I always listen to your voice and do your will with love.

Noah and the Ark

Genesis 6–9

Years passed. Adam and Eve had children who grew up and had children of their own. Over time, many people lived on the earth. These people did not obey God. They sinned and did many bad things. When God saw all the evil they did, he was sorry he had made them.

But one man still loved and obeyed God. His name was Noah. One day God told Noah that he was going to send a great flood. It would wash away all the evil in the world. God wanted to keep Noah and his family safe. So he told Noah to build an ark out of wood.

Noah believed God and did as God asked. When the ark was built, it was big enough to hold Noah, his family, and two of every kind of animal.

Then the rain started. It rained for forty days and forty nights. Water covered the whole world!

The only living things left were on the ark. Noah, his family, and the animals were all safe as the ark floated on the water.

After forty days the rain stopped. Noah opened a window in the ark and let out a raven. He hoped it would find dry land. But the bird soon returned without finding a place to land. A week later, Noah let out a dove. The dove came back with a small olive branch in its

beak. Noah knew this meant that
trees and bushes were growing some
place on dry ground!

Soon the ark came upon land.
God told Noah and his family to free
all the animals. Noah was so happy
to leave the ark. He thanked God for
keeping his family safe from the
flood.

15

God blessed Noah and his family. He put a bright rainbow in the sky as the sign of his promise, or *covenant*, never to flood the earth again.

"See," God said, "I have put my rainbow in the clouds to remind you of my covenant with you and all living things."

God, help us listen to you and obey what is right.

17

God's Promise to Abraham

Genesis 12:1–7; 17:1–16; 21:1–3

One day God told Abram, "Leave your home and go to a land that I will show you." Abram and his wife left right away. When they got to the land of Canaan, God told Abram, "I will give this land to your children." Abram did not have any children, and he and his wife were very old. But he hoped in God.

Time passed, and Abram still did not have children. Then God said to him,

"Your name is now Abraham. I will bless you and your wife with a baby boy."

God gave Abraham and his wife, Sarah, a son named Isaac. They were glad that God kept his promise.

You are a good Father to all your children, O God.

Jacob's Dream

Genesis 25:24–26, 29–34; 27:41–45; 28:12–22

Isaac and his wife, Rebekah, had twin boys. Esau was born first, and Jacob came next.

One day Esau was hungry and wanted some of Jacob's food. He said he would trade his birthright to Jacob for something to eat. (Because Esau was born first, he had a special place of honor in the family.)

Later Esau was sorry he traded his birthright. He was very angry, and Jacob had to run far away.

One night on his trip, Jacob had a dream. Stairs came down from heaven, and angels went up and down on them. Then

God told him, "I will bless you and be with you and your family." When Jacob woke up he was very happy. He knew that God would be with him always.

Lord, I know you are always with me.

Joseph and
the Coat of Many Colors

Genesis 37

Jacob had twelve sons, but he loved Joseph best. He gave the boy a coat of many bright colors. The brothers were jealous of Joseph and wanted to get rid of him.

One day when they were working in the fields, Joseph came to join them. This was their chance. They ripped off his coat and threw him into a dry, deep well. Reuben, the oldest brother, secretly planned to go back later and rescue Joseph. But before he could do so, traders on their way to Egypt stopped by. So the brothers sold Joseph as a slave to these men.

Lord, help me to not be jealous of my brothers and sisters.

23

Joseph in Egypt

Genesis 40; 41:1–45

Joseph had a special gift from God. "I can tell people what their dreams mean," he told one of the king's servants. Later the king (called Pharaoh) had a scary dream about skinny cows that ate fat cows. What could this mean? Pharaoh sent for Joseph at once.

Joseph listened as Pharaoh shared his dream. Then Joseph told him the dream meant that

food was going to run out in the land. If Egypt got things ready, there would be enough food for all. Pharaoh said, "I can tell that God is with you. You must take care of everything." And he put Joseph in charge.

Lord, I count on you to be with me in times of trouble.

25

Joseph and
His Brothers in Egypt

Genesis 41–43

When the food ran out, people from all over turned to Joseph for help.

Back home, Jacob heard that Egypt had extra food. He sent his sons there to buy some.

When the brothers saw Joseph, they did not know him. Joseph knew them but did not tell them who he was. He gave them food and sent them home.

Soon they ran out of food again. When they went back to Joseph, he said, "I am Joseph, your brother." They were afraid, but Joseph told them, "Do not worry. You sold me into slavery, but God used it to help people. Go and bring my father here. Bring your families too, for there is food for all."

O Lord, help me forgive
and help others.

27

Moses Is Born

Exodus 1; 2:1–10

In Egypt, Jacob and his family were known as Hebrews or Israelites.

Many years later, there was a new Pharaoh. He saw how many Hebrews there were and was afraid, so he made them slaves. He also gave an evil order:

28

"When a baby boy is born to the Israelites, throw him into the river. The girls may live."

One Hebrew family had a baby boy. They hid him in a basket near the river. His sister watched from the tall grass to see what would happen to him. Pharaoh's daughter came along. She heard the baby's cries and sent a servant to get him. She adopted the boy and named him Moses.

Lord, help me be good to every person, old and young.

29

Moses and the Burning Bush

Exodus 2:11–25; 3; 4

Moses grew up. One day he saw an Egyptian beating a Hebrew man. Moses was so angry, he killed the Egyptian and hid him in the sand. Then he ran away. Moses found a job taking care of sheep. He was watching them when he saw a bush on fire. As he came near it, a voice called out, "Moses! Moses!"

"Here I am," Moses said.

The voice went on, "I am God, and I want you to lead the Israelites out of Egypt."

Moses tried to tell God he was not the right person to do this. "I will be with you," God told him. So Moses went back to Egypt.

O God, help me
do what you ask of me.

31

Moses and Aaron
Go to Pharaoh

Exodus 5–10

God told Moses to take his brother Aaron with him to see Pharaoh. First they went to the Israelites and told them that God had heard their cries. Then they went to Pharaoh and said, "The God of Israel wants you to let his people go."

Pharaoh laughed and said, "Who is this god that I should obey him?"

God told Aaron to throw his staff to the ground, and it turned into a snake! Then Pharaoh's magicians threw down their staffs. They too became snakes, but Aaron's snake swallowed theirs. Then Aaron's snake turned back into a staff! Still, Pharaoh would not listen. He would not let God's people go.

Lord, help me listen when you are trying to show me what I must do.

33

The First Passover

Exodus 11–12:28

God tried many times to make Pharaoh let his people go. Pharaoh would just not listen. At last God told Moses that Pharaoh would soon send them away. But something terrible would take place first: every firstborn in the land would die.

God had a plan to make sure all the firstborn Hebrew children would be safe. He had the Hebrews mark their doors with lamb's blood. When the angel of the Lord saw the blood, he would pass over these houses. Everyone inside would be safe. That is why this special night is called Passover. It marks the night God freed his people from slavery.

I bless your name, O Lord.
You answer me when I call
for help.

35

The Red Sea

Exodus 12:29–15:22

Pharaoh told Moses and Aaron, "Take your people and leave at once!"

The Israelites hurried out of Egypt. Soon they came to the shore of the Red Sea. How would they get across? Even worse, Pharaoh had changed his mind. His army was on its way to take them back to Egypt!

Then God had Moses lift up his staff. The sea parted in two, with a dry path down the middle. The Israelites used it to cross to the other side. When Pharaoh's army chased after them, the water fell back into place. It covered over the army. The Israelites then sang and danced. They praised God who had saved them!

I praise you for all you have done for me, O Lord.

Manna from Heaven

Exodus 16

The Israelites did not have much food and water with them. Soon they were hungry and thirsty. They grew angry with Moses and Aaron.

"We should never have left Egypt," they said. "We had lots of food to eat there!"

Then God told Moses, "I have bread from heaven to give you."

That morning he sent manna, a food tasting like wafers made with honey. For water, God told Moses to strike a rock with his staff. When he did so, water came out.

God sent this special food every day to the Israelites until they came to the land God was leading them.

We turn to you, O God, to help us in every need!

The Ten Commandments

Exodus 19–20

The Israelites came to the desert of Sinai. There God called Moses to the top of a mountain and said, "Tell the Israelites: 'I have saved you from the hands of Pharaoh. If you keep my covenant, you will be my special people.'"

Then God gave Moses these rules or laws, which are called the Ten Commandments.

1. I am the Lord your God. You shall not have strange gods before me.
2. You shall not take the name of the Lord your God in vain.
3. Remember to keep holy the Lord's day.
4. Honor your father and your mother.
5. You shall not kill.
6. You shall not commit adultery.
7. You shall not steal.
8. You shall not bear false witness against your neighbor.
9. You shall not covet your neighbor's wife.
10. You shall not covet your neighbor's goods.

God, help me to keep your laws of love, the Ten Commandments.

Ruth and Naomi

Ruth 1–4

Years passed, and Moses died. God chose Joshua to lead the Israelites to the land of Canaan.

Once, when food ran out in the land, a family moved from Bethlehem to Moab. Then the father of the family and his two sons died. That left the man's wife, Naomi, alone with her sons' wives. Naomi was

very sad. She wanted to go home, and she tried to send her daughters-in-law to their families.

"I will not leave you," Ruth said. And she went back with Naomi.

In Bethlehem, Ruth met a kind man named Boaz. He let her pick grain in his field. Later Ruth became his wife, and they had a son. Naomi was happy again, because of her grandson, Obed.

God, bless all who need food or a place to live today.

43

God Calls Samuel

1 Samuel 1; 3:1–10

Hannah could not have children and prayed to God for a son. Eli, the prophet, heard about Hannah's troubles and blessed her.

"May God hear your prayer," he said.

Some time later, Hannah had a baby boy! She named him Samuel. When Samuel was old enough, she asked Eli to teach him about the Lord.

Once, when he was asleep, Samuel heard a voice call him. He went to Eli, but Eli had not called. So Samuel went back to sleep. This happened two more times. Then Eli knew it was the Lord calling. He told the boy what to say. When the Lord called again, Samuel said, "Speak, for I am listening!"

O God, help me to listen well to you.

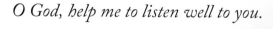

45

Saul Becomes King

1 Samuel 8–10

Samuel grew up, and the Lord was with him. He ruled the people well. When Samuel became old, he made his sons rulers in Israel. But Samuel's two sons were not like him. The people were not happy with them, so they went to Samuel and said, "We want a king to rule over us and fight our battles, like other nations have!"

Samuel turned to the Lord and asked him what to do.

"Give them a king," said the Lord. The Lord then chose Saul to lead his people. The people were happy when Saul became king of Israel. They called out, "Long live King Saul!"

God, you will show me the right way when I ask you.

David and Goliath

1 Samuel 16–17

It was time for a new king, so God sent Samuel out to find one. Samuel met Jesse's sons, one by one. With each son, Samuel thought, *This must be the Lord's chosen one.*

"No," the Lord said, "he is not the one I want."

After Samuel had met seven sons, he asked Jesse, "Do you have any more?"

"Only the youngest," Jesse said. "He is watching the sheep."

When David came, the Lord said to Samuel, "He is the one!" Then Samuel poured oil over David's head to show that God had picked him. And from that day the Lord was with David in a special way.

King Saul was sad. The Lord's spirit had left him because he did not listen to God. Only music helped Saul feel better. He sent for David, who played the harp for him.

49

At the time, the Philistines were fighting the Israelites. Goliath, one of the Philistines, said to them, "Pick one of your men to fight me. If he wins, we will be your slaves. If I win, you will be our slaves."

David was not afraid of Goliath. He told King Saul, "God saved me from bears and lions when I watched the sheep. He will save me from this Philistine!"

Then David went to face Goliath.
With his slingshot, David shot a stone
at Goliath and killed him.
David was a hero!

God, help me turn to you when I need help.

A Sign for Isaiah

Isaiah 7; 9 1–7

Isaiah was a great prophet. One day God sent him to King Ahaz to tell him not to be afraid. Israel's

enemies were going to attack, but God wanted Ahaz to know that the Lord was on Israel's side. No matter what, God would be with them. Then Isaiah told him about something that would take place one day: "A young woman will have a baby boy. She will name him Emmanuel," which means "God is with us."

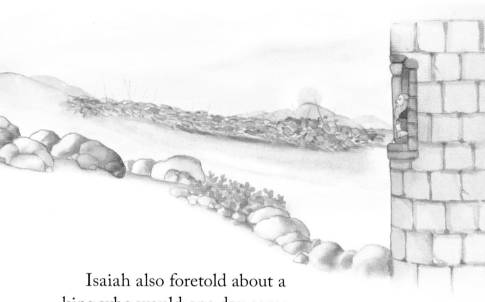

Isaiah also foretold about a king who would one day come from David's family. He would bring peace and be a light for all people.

God, may I show my trust in you by listening to your word with love.

Jonah and the Big Fish

Jonah 1–4

God told Jonah to go to the city of Nineveh. The people there were sinning, and God wanted Jonah to tell them to stop. But Jonah did not want to do this. So he got on a boat headed the other way.

That night God sent a storm on the sea. Jonah was asleep, so the sailors woke him and said, "The ship is going down! Ask God to save us!"

Jonah told them he was running away from God. The sailors did not know what to do, so Jonah had

them throw him into the water. When they did, the sea became calm.

Then God sent a giant fish to swallow Jonah! Jonah prayed from inside the fish's belly. After three days, God made the fish spit Jonah out on land.

At last Jonah went to Nineveh as God had asked. He told the people that God wanted them to change. And all the people listened to Jonah. They stopped sinning, and God forgave them.

But Jonah was angry. He said to God, "That is why I did not want to come here. I knew you would forgive them."

Jonah went and sat down. The sun was hot, and Jonah was glad when God sent a plant to shade him. But the next day the plant died, and Jonah was angry again. Then the Lord said, "You care about this plant that died. Is it not more important for me to care about these people?"

God, help me to be kind to everyone.

57

58

New Testament

An Angel Comes to Mary

Luke 1:26–38

One day God sent the Angel Gabriel to a young woman named Mary. The angel said, "Rejoice! The Lord is with you. You are blessed by God above all women!" Mary wondered why an angel would come to see her. Then Gabriel said, "Do not be afraid, Mary, for God is pleased with

you. You are going to have a son, and you will name him Jesus. He will rule over Israel forever."

Mary said, "I am not married, so how can I have a child?"

"The Holy Spirit will do this," Gabriel told her. "Your son will be truly the Son of God."

Mary said, "Yes, let this take place as you have said."

God, help me to always follow your will.

Jesus Is Born

Luke 2:1–20; Matthew 2:1–11

In those days a new law was made. The emperor of Rome wanted to know how many people there were and where they were from. So people had to go back to the city where they had been born to be counted.

62

Mary was now the wife of Joseph. Since Joseph was from David's family, it meant that Mary and Joseph had to go to Bethlehem, the city of David. It was a long trip. When they got to Bethlehem, all the inns were full. The only place they could find to stay in was a stable for animals. And it was there that Jesus was born.

The angels were full of joy. They went to shepherds in the fields and said, "We have great news! Today in Bethlehem your Savior has been born." Then the angels sang, "Glory to God in heaven, and peace to people on earth!"

After the angels left, the shepherds said to one another, "Let us go to see this for ourselves!" They found Mary and Joseph, with baby Jesus lying in the manger. It was just as the angels had told them.

Three wise men came from the East. They followed a star that they knew would lead them to a newborn king. When they came to the stable, they gave Jesus special gifts of gold, frankincense, and myrrh. Then they went back to their own countries.

With the angels I praise you, O Lord!

65

Jesus Is Found in the Temple

Luke 2:41–52

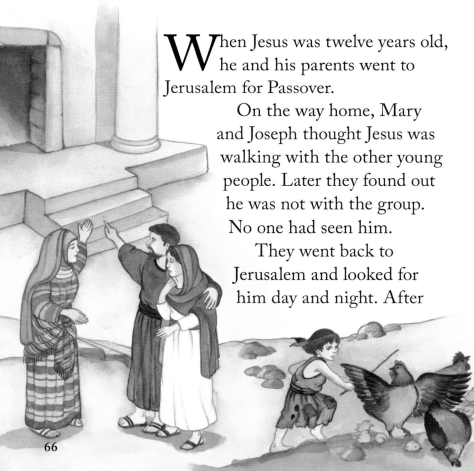

When Jesus was twelve years old, he and his parents went to Jerusalem for Passover.

On the way home, Mary and Joseph thought Jesus was walking with the other young people. Later they found out he was not with the group. No one had seen him.

They went back to Jerusalem and looked for him day and night. After

three days they found him in the Temple, talking with the Jewish teachers. These men could not believe how much Jesus knew about his faith.

Mary said to him, "We were looking for you all over town."

Jesus said, "Didn't you know I would be here in my Father's house?" And he went back home with his parents and obeyed them.

Lord, help me to always love and obey my parents.

68

The Baptism of Jesus

Matthew 3:1–17

John baptized people in the Jordan River. He told them how important it was to be sorry for their sins.

Jesus was now grown up. One day he went to the place where John was baptizing.

When John saw Jesus coming to him, he said, "I should not baptize you. You should baptize me!" John did not feel worthy to baptize Jesus. But Jesus told him, "We must follow God's plan." So John baptized Jesus.

As Jesus came up out of the water, a bright light shone down on him. Then a voice from heaven said, "This is my dear Son. I am pleased with him."

Lord, help me to please you in all that I do and say.

Jesus Calls the Apostles

Luke 5:1–10; 6:12–16

Jesus was teaching a crowd of people from a boat. When he was done, he said to Simon, a fisherman, "Let's go out into deep water. Then you can catch some fish."

"Teacher," Simon said, "we worked all night and did not catch anything. But if you say so, I will try again."

Then Simon and his friends caught a lot of fish!
When they were back on land, Simon knelt down and
said, "Lord, I am not worthy to follow you."

Jesus said, "Do not be afraid. From now on you
will catch people, not fish." Simon decided to leave
everything and follow Jesus.

Jesus called twelve men to be his Apostles. They
would learn everything from Jesus, and he would be
their teacher, or Rabbi.

Jesus, I want to learn all that you teach me.

71

The Wedding at Cana

John 2:1–12

There was a wedding in Cana. Jesus was there with his mother and disciples. At the party, Mary saw that something was wrong. There was no more wine to drink! She went and told Jesus. He said to her, "How does that concern me? It is not my time yet."

Then Mary told the waiters to go to Jesus. "Do whatever he tells you," she added.

Jesus sent them to fill six large jars with water. When the head waiter drank from one of these jars, he said, "This is really good wine!"

Jesus had changed the water into wine! This was his first miracle.

Jesus, I believe in you and trust all that you tell me to do.

The Our Father

Matthew 5:44–48; 6:5–13

People came to hear Jesus teach. He said, "Love those who are not kind to you. Love everyone like your Father in heaven loves them." Jesus also helped people learn how to pray. He said, "When you pray, you don't need a lot of words. Your Father already knows what you need." Then he told them, "Pray like this:

74

Our Father, who art in Heaven, hallowed be thy name. Thy kingdom come, thy will be done on earth as it is in heaven. Give us this day our daily bread, and forgive us our trespasses, as we forgive those who trespass against us. And lead us not into temptation, but deliver us from evil. Amen."

Father, help me to stay close to you always.

75

Jesus Cures
the Daughter of Jairus

Mark 5:21–24, 35–43

A man named Jairus told Jesus that his daughter was very sick.

"Please come to cure her!" he said. Jesus went with him right away.

When they got to the house, there were people outside. They told Jairus, "Your daughter is dead."

"She is only asleep," Jesus said, and the people laughed at him. Then Jesus turned to Jairus and said, "Do not be afraid, just trust." He went into the girl's room and took her hand into his. Then he said, "Get up, little girl." She opened her eyes at once and sat up! Her parents were so happy!

Jesus, help me remember that I never have to be afraid when you are near.

77

Jesus Multiplies
the Loaves and Fish

John 6:1–15

Many people came to listen to Jesus. When he was done teaching, he asked one of his disciples, Philip, "Where could we get food to feed everyone?"

"We could never have enough money to feed so many!" Philip said.

Then Jesus told everyone to sit down. A boy who was there had five loaves of bread and two fish. First Jesus blessed the bread and then gave it to the people to eat. He did the same with the fish. After everyone had eaten, they took up what was left over. There were twelve baskets of food left! It was a miracle!

Lord Jesus, I offer you all that I have. I want to help others with the gifts you have given me.

The Bread of Life

John 6:25–69

People came to Jesus looking for more food. They had seen the miracle of the loaves and fish. Jesus told them about food that never runs out.

"Lord," they said, "give us this kind of bread!"

Then Jesus said, "I am the bread of life that the Father sends you from heaven."

It was hard for people to understand these words. Jesus told them, "Whoever eats my flesh and drinks my blood will live forever."

Many people could not accept these words. They did not follow Jesus any more. But his disciples stayed with him. Simon Peter said, "We believe that you are the One sent by God."

Lord, I believe that the Father sent you
as the Bread of Life!

81

The Lost Son

Luke 15:11–32

Jesus told a story: "A father had two sons. The younger son said, 'Father, give me now the money that will come to me after you die.' So the father did. Then the son ran away. He spent all his money on wild parties.

"The son had no more money. He got a job taking care of pigs, but they had more to eat than he did! He decided to go home.

"The father saw him coming and ran to meet him. The son said, 'Father, I have sinned. I do not deserve to be your son.'

"But the father hugged him and said, 'Tonight we will have a party with the best food and drink!'

"Now the older son was out working. When he came home, he heard music and asked what was going on. Someone told him, 'Your brother has come back, safe and sound, and your father is very happy.'

"The older son was angry and would not go in. His father came out to talk to him. The older son said,

'I have worked hard for you all my life! Now your son comes back after wasting your money, and you throw a party?!'

"'Son,' his father said, 'all that I have is already yours. But we must celebrate. Your brother was dead, but now he is alive. He was lost, and now he is found.'"

Lord, help me remember that the Father always forgives us when we ask him to.

85

Jesus Raises Lazarus

John 11:1–44

Jesus was friends with Lazarus and his sisters Mary and Martha. They were from Bethany. One day, Jesus learned that his friend was sick. By the time he got to Bethany, Lazarus had died.

Martha said, "Lord, if you had been here, my brother would still be alive."

"Whoever believes in me will not die," Jesus told her. "Do you believe this?"

"Yes, Lord," Martha said. "I believe you are the Son of God."

Then they brought Jesus to the tomb where they had placed Lazarus. After Jesus prayed to his Father, he called out, "Lazarus, come out!" The dead man came out at once.

Jesus had performed a miracle and brought Lazarus back to life!

Jesus, I believe God sent you to give us eternal life.

Jesus Goes to Jerusalem

Matthew 21:1–11; Luke 19:39–40

Jesus and his disciples were going to Jerusalem for the Passover feast. Just before they got to the city, he called two disciples aside. He told them to go to a place where they would find a donkey. They were to bring it back for him to ride. When the disciples went to look for the donkey, it was just where he said it would be. They brought it back for Jesus. Then

he rode into Jerusalem, just as Scripture says: "Here comes your king, gentle and riding on a donkey."

Many people followed Jesus as he rode through the streets. They were happy to see him and called out, "Hosanna! Blessed is he who comes in God's name! Hosanna, Son of David!" The people cut branches from the trees and waved them as Jesus passed. They also spread their cloaks on the road in front of him. Many were there because they had heard what Jesus had done for Lazarus.

90

Once he was inside Jerusalem, the people of the city asked those who followed Jesus, "Who is this man?"

"This is the prophet Jesus," they said, "and he comes from Galilee!"

The religious leaders were not happy about all the noise. They told Jesus, "Tell your disciples to be quiet!"

Jesus said, "If they did not speak, the stones would cry out!"

O God, may I always praise you for your works!

The Last Supper

Luke 22:7–27

Jesus asked Peter and John to find a place for them to eat the Passover meal.

When they began the meal, Jesus told his disciples, "I have wanted so much to eat this supper with you." Taking some bread, he blessed it and broke it into pieces. "Take this bread," he said. "This is my body, which I am giving up for you." He also blessed a cup of wine. Then he passed it to them and said, "This is my blood, which I am giving for you."

The disciples were happy to share this special meal with Jesus. All were happy, that is, except for one man—Judas Iscariot. He would turn against Jesus.

After the meal, Jesus said, "One of you will hand me over to my enemies."

The disciples could not believe their ears! They asked one another, "Who would do such a thing?" Then they started to argue about which one of them was the most important.

Jesus said to them, "Who is greater, the one who is served at table or the one who serves? Is it not the one who is served? But here I am with you as the one who serves."

Jesus, I believe in your Real Presence. You give me your Body to eat and your Blood to drink in Holy Communion. Thank you, Lord!

Jesus Is Arrested

Luke 22:39–62

That night after supper, Jesus and his friends walked to the Mount of Olives. Jesus often went to pray there. He told his disciples to pray, then he went on ahead of them.

He prayed, "Father, if you want to, you can take this trial away from me. If not, may your will be done." Jesus knew that his enemies were coming. He was very sad. After he prayed some more, Jesus went back to the disciples and found them asleep.

Just then soldiers came up to him. Judas was leading them. He went up to Jesus and kissed him. This was the sign for the soldiers to arrest Jesus. They took him away and led him to the high priest's house.

Peter followed from behind. He warmed himself before a fire outside the house. A maid saw him and said, "This man was with Jesus."

"I do not know him," Peter replied.

A while later, someone else said, "Aren't you one of the disciples?" Again Peter said no.

An hour later, someone else said, "This man must have been with Jesus. He is from Galilee!" Peter was afraid and shouted, "I don't know him!"

Then a rooster crowed, and Peter remembered that Jesus had told him that he would deny knowing Jesus three times. When he remembered this Peter cried because he was sorry.

Jesus, give me the courage to always say that I believe in you and love you.

99

Jesus Dies on the Cross

Matthew 27; Mark 15; Luke 23; John 18:28–19:42

Jesus was put on trial. His enemies told lies about him. Jesus had done no wrong, but the judge still ordered the soldiers to crucify him.

The soldiers made fun of Jesus. They put a purple cloak around his

shoulders and a crown of thorns on his head. They slapped him and cried out, "Hail to the King!" Then they led Jesus to Calvary to be crucified. As he walked, Jesus carried a heavy Cross through the streets.

As Jesus walked, he grew weaker. The soldiers were afraid that he would die on the way. So they made Simon from Cyrene help Jesus carry his Cross.

Many people came out to see what was going on. They felt sorry for the kind teacher. Women were crying because of what was happening to Jesus.

When they got to Calvary, the soldiers hung Jesus on the Cross. They crucified him between two thieves. Jesus loved us to the end. He died for all people. Among his last words were: "Father, forgive these people. They do not know what they are doing."

After Jesus died, a disciple named Joseph came to bury his body. Disciples took Jesus down from the Cross and placed his body in a new tomb made out of rock. They put a heavy stone in front of the tomb. Then they went home.

Jesus, you forgave those who crucified you. You forgive us. Help me to forgive those who hurt me.

Jesus Is Alive!

John 20:1–18

Early on Sunday morning, Mary Magdalene went to the tomb. She was a follower of Jesus and had stood by the Cross of Jesus, with his Mother and one of his disciples.

When Mary got to the tomb, she saw that the stone had been rolled to one side! She ran back to tell Jesus' friends what had happened. Peter and another disciple ran to the tomb. They saw that it was just as Mary Magdalene had said. Then they went home.

Mary stayed near the tomb, crying. Where was Jesus' body? She looked inside, and she saw two angels! They asked her, "Why are you crying?"

Mary said, "Someone has taken away my Lord, and I don't know where he is!"

She turned around and saw a man standing there. It was Jesus, but she did not recognize him. She thought he was a gardener. He said, "Woman, why are you crying? Who are you looking for?"

"Sir," she said, "if you know where they have put Jesus, please tell me and I will take him away."

Then he called her by name, "Mary!"

She turned to him and said, "Teacher!"

Jesus told her, "Go and tell my brothers, 'I am going back to my Father and your Father, to my God and your God.'"

Jesus, I believe that you rose from the dead!

107

Jesus Breaks Bread with Two Disciples

Luke 24:13–35

Two disciples were walking to a town called Emmaus. They were sad that Jesus had died. Could he really be alive, as some of the disciples said? As they walked, another man came along. It was Jesus, but they did not recognize him. He asked what they were talking about. They said, "Are you the only one who

has not heard?" And they told him about Jesus, how they had hoped Jesus was the Messiah, and how he had been crucified and was dead. When they were done, Jesus said, "Didn't Christ have to suffer so that he could enter into his glory?" Then he explained the Scriptures that spoke about the Messiah.

At Emmaus, they sat down to eat. When Jesus broke the bread, they knew him! Then he vanished. They said to one another, "We should have known! Our hearts were on fire as he spoke!"

Jesus, may I always recognize you at Mass—
in your word and in the Sacred Host.

Jesus Goes Up to Heaven

Acts 1:1–14

The disciples saw Jesus for forty days after he rose from the dead. He taught them all about the kingdom of God. When it was time for Jesus to go back to his Father, he told them, "The Holy Spirit will make you my witnesses to the ends of the world."

After he said this, Jesus went up to heaven. The disciples stood looking up at the sky. Then two angels came and asked them, "Why are you staring up at the clouds? Don't worry. Jesus will come back again, in the same way that you just saw him go up to heaven."

Jesus, help me witness to you in all that I do today.

The Holy Spirit Comes

Acts 2

The disciples were praying with Mary, the Mother of Jesus. All of a sudden a very strong wind blew through the house. Bright flames of fire came down and danced over each one's head. All were filled with the Holy Spirit. The disciples could speak in different languages, for the Spirit wanted everyone to understand God's message.

At that time there were people from different nations in Jerusalem. When the disciples spoke about Jesus, the people were amazed. Each one could understand what the disciples said in his or her own language!

Then Peter told them the good news about Jesus. Many people came to believe. About 3,000 persons were baptized that day!

Come, Holy Spirit, fill us with the fire of your love!

113

Come, Lord Jesus!

Revelation 22

In the last book of the Bible, Jesus tells us, "I am coming soon. Happy are those who keep my word! Let whoever is thirsty come to me, and I will give them life-giving water."

With all people who believe, I pray, "Come, Lord Jesus!"

114

For the Church

Heavenly Father, I pray for the Catholic Church, made up of people around the world who belong to you in Baptism. I pray for the pope, bishops, and the priests of my diocese. I pray for religious priests, brothers, and sisters who pray for and serve the Church in so many ways. I pray for my family and all those who have helped me learn about my faith. And I pray for all Catholics in my parish and in the world that we may be faithful and compassionate toward one another. Help all of us to follow Jesus, your beloved Son, with our whole hearts and share his love with everyone we meet. Amen.

Who are the Daughters of St. Paul?

We are Catholic sisters. Our mission is to be like Saint Paul and tell everyone about Jesus! There are so many ways for people to communicate with each other. We want to use all of them so everyone will know how much God loves us. We do this by printing books (you're holding one!), making radio shows, singing, helping people at our bookstores, using the internet, and in many other ways.

VISIT OUR WEB SITE AT WWW.PAULINE.ORG

Pauline
BOOKS & MEDIA

The Daughters of St. Paul operate book and media centers
at the following addresses. Visit, call, or write the one nearest
you today, or find us at www.paulinestore.org.

CALIFORNIA
3908 Sepulveda Blvd, Culver City, CA 90230   310-397-8676
3250 Middlefield Road, Menlo Park, CA 94025   650-369-4230

FLORIDA
145 SW 107th Avenue, Miami, FL 33174   305-559-6715

HAWAII
1143 Bishop Street, Honolulu, HI 96813   808-521-2731

ILLINOIS
172 North Michigan Avenue, Chicago, IL 60601   312-346-4228

LOUISIANA
4403 Veterans Memorial Blvd, Metairie, LA 70006   504-887-7631

MASSACHUSETTS
885 Providence Hwy, Dedham, MA 02026   781-326-5385

MISSOURI
9804 Watson Road, St. Louis, MO 63126   314-965-3512

NEW YORK
115 E. 29th Street, New York City, NY 10016   212-754-1110

SOUTH CAROLINA
243 King Street, Charleston, SC 29401   843-577-0175

TEXAS
No book center; for parish exhibits or outreach evangelization, contact:
210-569-0500 or SanAntonio@paulinemedia.com or P.O. Box 761416,
San Antonio, TX 78245

VIRGINIA
1025 King Street, Alexandria, VA 22314   703-549-3806

CANADA
3022 Dufferin Street, Toronto, ON M6B 3T5   416-781-9131